Brian McBride

Soccer Star

Joanne Mattern

Mitchell Lane
PUBLISHERS

P.O. Box 196
Hockessin, Delaware 19707
Visit us on the web: www.mitchelllane.com
Comments? email us: mitchelllane@mitchelllane.com

Printing   1   2   3   4   5   6   7   8

A Robbie Reader
No Hands Allowed

Brandi Chastain   **Brian McBride**   DaMarcus Beasley
David Beckham   Freddy Adu   Josh Wolff
Landon Donovan

Library of Congress Cataloging-in-Publication Data
Mattern, Joanne, 1963-
    Brian McBride : by Joanne Mattern.
        p. cm. – (A Robbie reader. No hands allowed)
    Includes bibliographical references and index.
    ISBN 1-58415-389-X (library bound)
1. McBride, Brian, 1972 – Juvenile literature. 2. Soccer players – United States – Biography – Juvenile literature. I. Title. II. Series.
GV942.7.M393M38 2006
796.334'092–dc22

                                                                        2005012780

ABOUT THE AUTHOR: Joanne Mattern is the author of more than 100 nonfiction books for children. Along with biographies, she has written extensively about animals, nature, history, sports, and foreign cultures. She lives near New York City with her husband and three young daughters.

PHOTO CREDITS: Cover– Globe Photos/Clinton H. Wallace; pp. 1, 3 – Jonathan Daniel/ Getty Images; p. 4– Stu Forster/Getty Images; p. 6 – AP Photo/Tony Gutierrezz; p. 8 – Globe Photos/Clinton H. Wallace; p. 11 – Jamie Kondrchek; p. 12 – Jonathan Daniel/ Allsport; p. 14 Andy Lyons/Getty Images p. 16 – AP Photo/John Todd; p. 18 – Al Bello/ Allsport; p. 20 – AP Photo/Terry Gilliam; p. 22 Jamie Kondrchek; p. 24 – AP Photo/Jay LaPrete; p. 26 – Jonathan Daniel/Getty Images

ACKNOWLEDGMENTS: The following story has been thoroughly researched, and to the best of our knowledge, represents a true story. While every possible effort has been made to ensure accuracy, the publisher will not assume liability for damages caused by inaccuracies in the data, and makes no warranty on the accuracy of the information contained herein. This story has not been authorized nor endorsed by Brian McBride nor anyone associated with Brian McBride.

TABLE OF CONTENTS

Brian, who is a striker for the Fulham soccer team in England, jumps high to move the ball. This action took place during a game between the Bolton Wanderers and Fulham at the Reebok Stadium in 2005 in Bolton, England.

A FRIGHTENING DISCOVERY

Playing soccer is Brian McBride's favorite thing to do. In September 2000, he was playing for a **professional** (pruh-FEH-shuh-nuhl) team in England. Brian was having a great time. He was playing very well. The fans liked him.

One night, Brian finished a game with his team. He felt good. Then he noticed something strange. There was a big lump in his armpit. His arm was swelling fast. Something was very wrong.

Brian went to the doctor. The doctor said he had a blood clot in his upper arm. Brian had to have an operation right away. He could not play soccer any more that year.

Mexico's Manuel Vidrio (left) goes for the ball against Brian during the 2002 World Cup second-round playoffs. The game was played at Jeonju World Cup Stadium in Jeonju, South Korea, in June 2002.

Brian had more medical problems the next year. He had another blood clot in his right arm. He had to have a serious operation to solve the problem. Doctors had to remove one of his ribs to relieve the pressure on his veins. Brian was very sick. Some people said he would never play soccer again. The thought made Brian very sad. He decided to do whatever he had to in order to play the sport he loved so much.

Finally, the doctors gave Brian good news. The operation had worked. Brian would not have any more blood clots. The doctors told him he could do anything he wanted. Best of all, he could rejoin his soccer team!

By 2002, Brian McBride was playing **professional** soccer again. He went on to continue his successful career both in the United States and in England. He also got married and became a father.

Getting sick was a scary experience for Brian. But he refused to let his illness stop him from achieving his goals. After his illness, Brian's life became better than ever.

7

This is a picture of Brian photographed at the Honda Player of the Year Award Ceremony in October 2003. He was a first-time finalist for the award.

FUN AND GAMES

Brian McBride was born on June 19, 1972, in Arlington Heights, Illinois. Arlington Heights is a small town near Chicago. Brian's parents are Maddie and Matthew McBride. Brian's dad worked as an advertising sales representative. Brian has an older brother named Matt and a younger sister named Megan.

Brian's parents were divorced when he was four years old. Mrs. McBride often had to work three jobs in order to make enough money to support the family. Still, Brian and his brother and sister always felt loved.

Brian loved sports and was very good at them. He often spent so much time playing that

he did not do his schoolwork. "I never really tried at school," Brian said. "I always thought that sports came first."

Brian started playing soccer when he was eight years old. He bounced the ball off his knees. He practiced dribbling the ball around

This is St. Louis University in St. Louis, Missouri. Brian attended college here.

the trees in his yard. Dribbling is using the feet to move the ball. He often got in trouble for dribbling the ball up and down the stairs of his house!

Soccer and baseball were Brian's favorite sports at Buffalo Grove High School. But Brian had a problem. His baseball coach wanted him to practice during the summer. So did his soccer coach. Brian decided that soccer would be his main sport. He went on to lead his high school team to the 1988 Illinois State Championship.

Brian had never been very serious about school. But he wanted to get a soccer **scholarship** (SKAH-luhr-ship) so he could play in college. That meant he had to work hard during his senior year of high school. "While everyone else was slacking off, I was playing soccer and studying harder than anybody to make sure that I got my grades right," he said.

Brian's hard work paid off. He won a scholarship to St. Louis University in St. Louis, Missouri. In 1990, Brian went to college. His adventures in soccer were just beginning.

Brian runs down the field with the ball during a game in April 1997 against the Dallas Burn at Ohio Stadium in Columbus, Ohio. The Columbus Crew won the game 2-1.

FROM COLLEGE TO THE CREW

Brian was one of the best soccer players at St. Louis University. He was named an All-American player in 1992 and 1993. He was also a runner-up for the Hermann Award in 1993. This award is given to the best college soccer player in the country. When Brian graduated in 1994, he was St. Louis University's all-time leading scorer. He also held the school records for the most goals and **assists** (uh-SISTS).

Brian wanted to be a **professional** soccer player. However, there was no **professional** soccer **league** (LEEG) in the United States at that time. Brian spent the 1994-1995 season

A happy Brian holds up his Most Valuable Player Award after the Major League Soccer All-Star Game. The game was part of the MLS All-Star Weekend in Orlando, Florida, in August 1998.

playing in Wolfsburg, Germany. Brian liked getting paid to play soccer. He was disappointed that his teammates did not really love the game. Brian said, "You weren't supposed to be happy. You were supposed to be doing your job." That just wasn't Brian's style!

Soon, Brian was thrilled to hear that an American **professional** soccer league was starting. Major League Soccer's first draft was held in 1996. During the draft, each team took turns picking players. Brian was the very first player to be chosen! He was selected by the Columbus (Ohio) Crew.

During his first season, Brian was the Crew's best scorer. He scored 17 goals and three assists for 37 points. He was one of only three players to score a goal against every team in the league.

Other players and league **officials** (uh-FISH-uhlz) enjoyed Brian's talent. A soccer official named Ivan Gazidis (gah-ZEE-dis) said, "Brian is one of the truly talented American

Brian (right) and China's Li Weifeng battle for the ball as Qi Honh looks on during a game in California in 2001.

players, and to have him swear **allegiance** (uh-LEE-juhns) to our league means a lot."

Brian had great seasons in 1997 and 1998 too. He was also chosen to be part of the United States World Cup Soccer Team in those years. The World Cup team plays against other teams from all over the world. In 1998, Brian scored the only U. S. goal at the World Cup tournament in France.

By then, Brian was considered to be the best U. S. player in the air. Fans loved to watch this powerful player jump up and head the ball toward the goal.

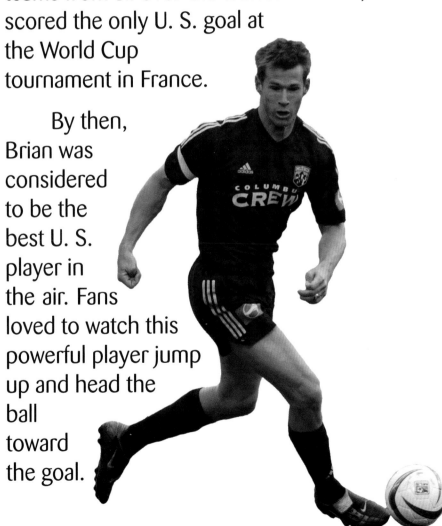

This photo shows Brian of Team USA in action against Team Mexico for the Nike Cup at Giants Stadium in East Rutherford, New Jersey, in June 2000. Team USA defeated Team Mexico 2-0.

HARD TIMES

During 1999 and 2000, Brian scored many goals for both the Crew and the U. S. World Cup Team. However, he also faced serious injuries during those years. On May 9, 1999, Brian jumped to head the ball against San Jose player Jamie Clark. Jamie's head hit Brian on the left side of his face and broke Brian's cheekbone. Brian had to have an operation to fix his face. "My doctor cut underneath my eye and went up through my mouth so I don't have any scars, and then inserted three plates," he explained.

On June 17, 2000, another player's elbow hit Brian in the right cheek. Once again, Brian

19

had to have an operation. This time, he missed six weeks of the season. He rejoined the Crew in time for the All-Star Game.

During the off-season, Brian went to England to play soccer. In England, soccer is called football, and it is very popular. English fans loved Brian just as much as American fans did.

Brian holds his wife Dina's hand during a news conference in January 2004 in Columbus, Ohio. Brian believes that his illness happened in order to bring Dina into his life.

However, Brian's medical problems continued. This was the period when he had his two blood clots. After his first operation, he went back home to Arlington Heights to recover. There, he met a woman named Dina Lundstrom. Brian and Dina had known each other when they were much younger. Dina's dad had been Brian's baseball coach!

Brian and Dina spent a lot of time together. Dina had just gotten divorced. She had a young daughter named Ashley. Brian and Dina got married in February, 2002.

Brian believes that his illness happened in order to bring Dina into his life. "What could have been a really negative thing, staying home as I recovered, turned out to be the most important thing ever in my life," he said. Brian McBride always tries to look on the bright side.

This photograph shows Brian controlling the ball. He is known for his skill in moving the ball while keeping it away from the other team.

MOVING ON AND GIVING BACK

Brian rejoined the Columbus Crew in 2002. He also continued to add his talents to the U. S. World Cup Team. In 2002, Brian went to Japan and South Korea to play in the World Cup matches. Brian scored game-winning goals against Portugal and Mexico to lead the U. S. team into the **quarter-finals** (KWOR-tur FY-nuhlz) against Germany. Unfortunately, the U. S. team lost a close game and was eliminated. But Brian became the first American to score in two different World Cups.

Brian played for the Columbus Crew through the 2003 season. Many English teams wanted Brian to play for them. In January,

2004, he signed a **contract** (KON-trakt) with a team in Fulham, England.

Playing in England meant big changes for Brian's family. In July 2003, Dina gave birth to a

Brian carries his daughters Ashley, right, and Ella, left, around the field. Meanwhile, fans celebrate the U.S. win over Grenada in the World Cup qualifier in June 2004.

daughter, Ella. In 2004, Brian, Dina, Ashley, and Ella moved to London. At first, the move was hard. Brian said the first year was "a bit of a shock for all of us." Everyone was homesick. But things got better as the family settled into their new home.

Brian is not just a star soccer player. He also tries to help others. In 2000, he became the first spokesperson for the Central Ohio **Diabetes** (dy-uh-BEE-teez) Association, or CODA. Helping this charity was important to Brian. His grandfather had died of diabetes. Dina's father also suffers from the disease.

Brian donates, or gives, one hundred dollars to CODA for every goal he scores and every game his team wins. His success means that he donates several thousand dollars to CODA every year.

Soccer has taken Brian McBride around the world. He would love to see soccer become as popular in America as it is in England. Meanwhile, he enjoys being part of English soccer. In 2005, Brian said, "I'm happy! I'm just happy to be a part of this team and whatever

job the coach asks of me, I'll do it." That attitude has made Brian McBride a star on and off the field.

Brian slides while attempting to keep the ball in play during a game against Poland in Chicago in 2004. Poland and the U.S. tied 1-1.

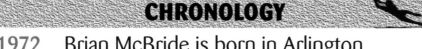

CHRONOLOGY

1972   Brian McBride is born in Arlington Heights, Illinois, on June 19.

1976   Brian's parents divorce.

1980   Brian begins to play soccer.

1988   Brian leads his high school team to the Illinois State Championship.

1990   Brian graduates from Buffalo Grove High School. He attends St. Louis University on a soccer scholarship.

1992   Brian is named an All-American player.

1993   Brian is named an All-American player for the second time. He is a runner-up for the Hermann Award, given to the best college soccer player in the country.

1994   Brian graduates from St. Louis University. He is the school's all-time leading scorer.

1994   Brian plays with a professional soccer team in Wolfsburg, Germany.

1996   The Columbus Crew drafts Brian.

1998   Brian scores the only U.S. goal at the World Cup in France.

1999 Brian breaks his left cheekbone during a game and requires surgery.

2000 Brian becomes spokesman for CODA in March and begins donating $100 for every goal he scores and every game his team wins. In July, Brian breaks his right cheekbone and has another surgery. Three months later, he has a blood clot in his upper arm and has yet another surgery.

2001 Brian has surgery to remove another blood clot.

2002 Brian marries Dina Lundstrom. He leads the U.S. team to the quarter-finals in the World Cup.

2003 Brian and Dina have a daughter, Ella.

2004 In January, Brian joins the Fulham Football Club in England.

2005 Brian plays in the MLS All-Star Game.

allegiance (uh-LEE-juhns)—loyalty.

assists (uh-SISTS)—helping other players score goals.

contract (KON-trakt)—a legal agreement between people or organizations.

diabetes (dy-uh-BEE-teez)—a disease in which the body does not produce enough insulin, leading to too much sugar in the blood.

league (LEEG)—a group of sports teams.

officials (uh-FISH-uhlz)—people who hold important positions in an organization.

professional (pruh-FEH-shuh-nuhl)—someone who is paid for a job.

quarter-finals (KWOR-tur FY-nuhlz)—games played among the last eight teams in a competition.

scholarship (SKAH-luhr-ship)—money given to someone to pay for school.

Books

Crisfield, Deborah W. *The Everything Kids Soccer Book: Rules, Techniques, and More About Your Favorite Sport!* Avon, Massachusetts: Adams Media Corporation, 2002.

Edom, Helen and Mike Osborne. *Starting Soccer.* Tulsa, Oklahoma: E. D. C. Publishing, 1999.

Herzog: Brad. *K Is for Kick: A Soccer Alphabet.* Farmington Hills, Michigan: Thomson Gale, 2003.

Hornby, Hugh. *Eyewitness: Soccer.* New York: D. K. Children, 2000.

Maccarone, Grace. *Soccer Game!* New York: Cartwheel Books, 1994.

Marzollo, Jean and Blanche Sims. *Soccer Sam.* New York: Random House Books for Young Readers, 1987.

Newspaper and Magazine Articles

Fields-Meyers, Thomas and Lorna Grisby. "Big Foot." *People*, June 3, 2002, p. 161.

Fifield, Dominic. "Charity Begins at Home for Flush McBride." *The Guardian Unlimited*, January 20, 2003. http://football.guardian.co.uk/ Match_Report/0,1527,-41236,00.html

Friedman, Nick. "Heading The Ball With Brian McBride." *Sports Illustrated for Kids*, September 1, 2002.

"The Life of Brian." Fulham Football Club News Detail, March 10, 2005. http://www.fulhamfc.com/ news/displaynews.asp?id_6051

Miller, Rusty. "McBride to Leave Columbus Crew, Join Fulham." The State.com, January 20, 2004. http://www.thestate.com/mld/thestate/sports/ 7753191.htm

Whiteside, Kelly. "Healthy McBride likely to start in World Cup." *USA Today*, May 6, 2002. http://www.usatoday.com/sports/soccer/ national/2002-05-07-mcbride-healthy.htm

On the Internet

Columbus Crew
http://columbus.crew.mlsnet.com/MLS/coc/ index.jsp

Fulham Football Club
http://www.fulhamfc.com

Soccer Times: Profile: Brian McBride
http://www.soccertimes.com/usteams/roster/ men/mcbride.htm

United States National Soccer Players Association: Brian McBride
http://www.ussoccerplayers.com/players/ brian_mcbride/

Yahoo! Sport: Brian McBride Football Profile
http://uk.sports.yahoo.com/fo/profiles/ 4986.html